ALICIA CZECHOWSKI

GOOD WITHOUT GOD

ATHEIST COLORING BOOK - QUOTES & SAYINGS

Pitchstone Publishing

Pitchstone Publishing
www.pitchstonepublishing.com

Good Without God: Atheist Coloring Book—Quotes & Sayings
Copyright © 2017 Alicia Czechowski
All Rights Reserved

ISBN: 9781939578303

Printed in the United States of America

Whether you live in Akron or Auckland, Youngstown or York, religion is foisted upon you, by friends, family, neighbors, and even society at large. I designed this coloring book, *Good Without God*, as a diverting antidote to such ubiquitous and gratuitous piety.

I have illustrated a variety pack of favorite English-language atheistic quotes and quips—poetic, philosophical, practical, and humorous. My aim has been to make a visual synonym for each quotation. I hope that readers-cum-colorers will be inspired, tickled, and motivated by these illustrated words of wit and wisdom and godlessness.

Who is proof against the profoundly touching reason contained in Douglas Adams' words, "Isn't it enough to see that a garden is beautiful without having to believe that there are fairies at the bottom of it, too?"

In the beginning.

Man

created.

God.

Isn't it enough
to See
that a Garden
is Beautiful
without
having to Believe
that there are
Fairies
at the
Bottom of it, too?
Douglas Adams

IMAGINE
NO RELIGION

JOHN LENNON

When one person
suffers from a delusion
it is called insanity

When many people
suffer from a delusion
it is called religion

Robt. M. Pirsig

I'd
take
the awe
of understanding

over
the awe of
ignorance
any day

Douglas Adams

RELIGION
IS LIKE a BLIND MAN LOOKING in a BLACK ROOM FOR a BLACK CAT THAT ISN'T THERE

and finding it.

OSCAR WILDE

REASON

is a Virtue

RELIGION is a VIRUS OF THE MIND

RICHARD DAWKINS

Is God willing
to prevent evil,
but not able?
  Then he is not omnipotent.
  Is he able, but not willing?
  Then he is malevolent.
  Is he both able and willing?
  Then whence cometh evil?
  Is he neither able
nor willing?
  Then why
call him God?

Epicurus

I QUESTION EVERYTHING

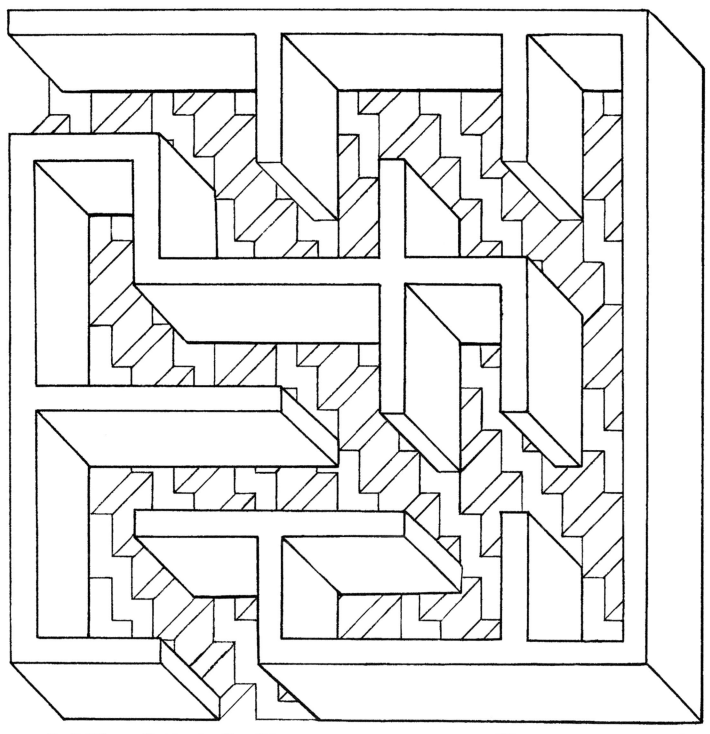

AND WORSHIP NOTHING

FAITH is BELIEF without EVIDENCE

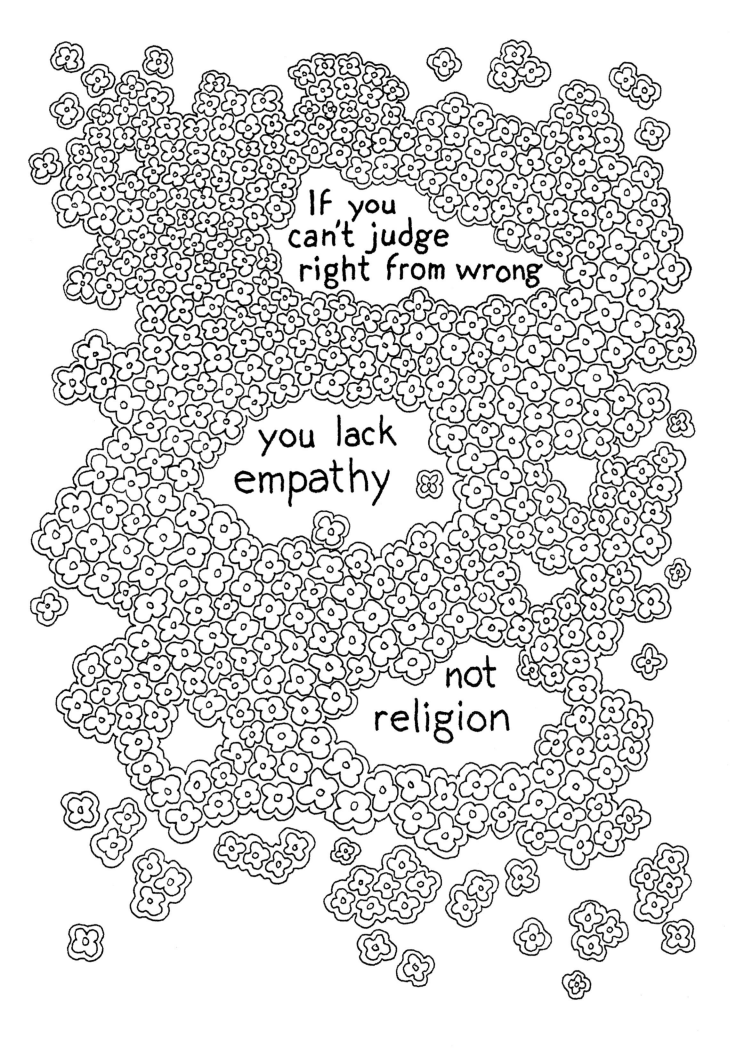